EASY BREEZY
Miracle

SECOND EDITION

A POWERFUL, EXCITING & SIMPLE GUIDE
TO CREATING AN EXTRAORDINARY LIFE

EASY BREEZY
Miracle

**A POWERFUL, EXCITING & SIMPLE GUIDE
TO CREATING AN EXTRAORDINARY LIFE**

EMMANUEL DAGHER

SECOND EDITION

Easy Breezy Miracle
A Powerful, Exciting & Simple Guide to Creating an Extraordinary Life

Emmanuel Dagher

Second Edition
Copyright © 2014 Emmanuel Dagher
Includes content from the First Edition © 2012

ISBN-13: 978-1492960973
ISBN-10: 1492960977

Cover Photo & Artwork by Magnified Manifesting, Inc.
Book Design by Lighthouse24

www.emmanueldagher.com

This book is dedicated to my family for navigating through life with an open mind and heart. I feel deeply blessed for the overflow of love and support they have given to me throughout my life.

I also dedicate this book to you, the reader, for your willingness to create even more miracles in your life. There's something very special to be said about the fact that you have been guided to a book like Easy Breezy Miracle.

*...blessed with
the energy of miracles...*

Foreword

I have known Emmanuel Dagher for several years now as a friend, teacher, and healer. Before we met, a friend told me about a spiritual group that she participated in of which Emmanuel was a member. She told me that he was the only person in the group with whom she felt a soul connection or kinship and she felt that I would really like him too. Later, when I joined that group and before we were introduced, I knew that Emmanuel had to be the person of whom my friend had spoken. The instant we officially met, Emmanuel became my younger spiritual "brother from another mother."

As the group meetings came to an end, Emmanuel and I formed our own group. We met regularly to talk about our life goals and to support one another in our spiritual practice. We became our own "two or more gathered" and created miracles together.

Emmanuel was the first to convince me that I could help facilitate healings for others. He encouraged me and reminded me of my own potential to be a miracle worker in my life and in the lives of others. It still surprises and amazes me that Emmanuel carries such wisdom and inspiration along with such youthfulness and humility. He inspires people to embrace the miracle of their very being.

Now, in reading this book, we all have the opportunity to remember the miracle that life itself is. We have the opportunity to prepare ourselves to welcome miracles into our lives on a consistent basis. We have the opportunity to awaken the miracle worker within each of us and, in doing so, to usher forth a miraculous shift in consciousness on this planet. With Emmanuel as our guide and facilitator, we have the practical, spiritual tools available to us to do all of these things with ease and with grace.

Let the journey begin. May we be astounded by the miracles that unfold before us.

Kim Mitchell

Contents

Orientation

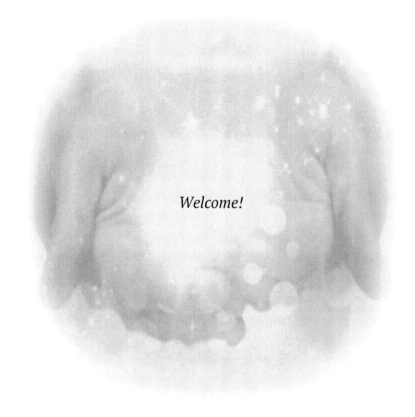

Welcome!

Introduction

Welcome, my miraculous friend! You hold in your hands the fruit of more than a decade of dedication to and passion for the healing arts. I am deeply honored and thrilled that you have been guided to this book, which I have put together for me to be able share with you some fun, simple, and exciting ways to attract miracles to all areas of your life.

In my joyful years of working (I call it "playing") as Miracle Coach and Holistic Healing Practitioner, I connected with thousands of people from all over the world who had sought some kind of transformation. Some of them had no idea where to begin or even what to look for, while others had already begun their personal journeys through reading an abundance of spiritual literature and self-empowerment books. But as diverse as my clients who shared their lives with me were, they seemed to always come upon a similar obstacle: although great wisdom and insight were beneficial, they never seemed to be enough. Whether or not they had been exposed to spiritual books and teachings, they always longed for a guide that was practical; a how-to manual on attracting transformations and positive experiences that were more palpable.

In this day and age, miracles are no longer considered airy-fairy wishful thinking. We find ourselves at a turning point in human history where science and spirituality are merging. Quantum Physics shows us that we, and everything around us, are pure energy. The funny thing is that science seems to have only recently caught up with spirituality, which has always been concerned with energies that we, as spiritual beings, project and receive. What we should be conscious of are the energies that we choose to dial into. When we choose to open ourselves to energies of love, gratitude, and joy, we magnify the possibilities of bringing forth our greatest vision of our lives into our experience; by receiving these energies, we allow ourselves to also project them.

Back to the feedback I was receiving from my clients who were craving for a simple guide to attracting positive transformation in their lives. When I hear something being shared with me many times over, I take notice. I see it as a kind of confirmation from the Universe. With all this in mind, *Easy Breezy Miracle* was birthed. I have written this special book to be your very own how-to manual, so that you can have easy access to powerful processes that will assist you in attracting miracles to yourself, and even to everyone around you.

I am absolutely certain that by integrating just some of the miracle processes provided for you in this book, you will begin to attract more miracles and blessings into your life. Make them a part of your everyday personal practice; and, more importantly, have fun! It makes my heart sing to see others create the kind of life they desire most for themselves.

Are you ready to create more miracles?

Before we begin, let's set an intention together for this book. let's open up to the energy of miracles by affirming out loud 3 times the following:

I am open and receptive to even more blessings & miracles in my life.

I am open and receptive to even more blessings & miracles in my life.

I am open and receptive to even more blessings & miracles in my life. And so it is!

Do you remember watching the Disney movie *Mary Poppins* as a child? Did you notice how miracles and blessings seemed to follow Mary everywhere she went, to the point that even when others were in her presence, they too would have the opportunity to experience the same miracles for themselves? The movie *Mary Poppins* is an easy, breezy way to explain the structure of this book, which is based on my two-fold approach for attracting miracles: miracle foundations, and miracle processes. Simply put, they can be thought of as theory and practice. I will elaborate on this later in the book though; for now, let me draw your attention to a wonderfully simple yet profound classic.

I remember having some powerful "aha!" moments while watching the movie *Mary Poppins* as a child. The first of two "aha!" moments I can clearly remember was inspired by Mary's demeanor throughout the movie. She always seemed to have an innate knowing that she could create miracles simply by intending for them to happen. She never doubted or worried whether or not they could happen. It seemed as if she fully trusted the Universe, and with that trust there was no room for second guessing. It seemed as though she was aligned with the Universe, hence attracting miracles was easy and expected.

I feel blessed to have cultivated my own demeanor of positive energy. I remain open and aligned to the magic and wonder life has to offer, and I am deeply grateful to my amazing parents who allowed me to do this. I know many parents tell their children that by using their imagination and believing in miracles, they are setting themselves up for disappointment. To me, this is a mindset driven by fear, and I feel blessed to have not experienced this. I understand this is just a parent's way of protecting their children, but protection shouldn't mean always limiting yourself to four walls. Thinking outside the box has allowed me to attract an overflow of miracles into my life that would have been blocked otherwise, and I encourage you to recognize your own box, and tear it down.

My second "aha!" moment was inspired by Mary's magical bag.

The first time I watched *Mary Poppins* and saw Mary pull out a large plant and an even larger coat rack from her tiny little bag, my mind immediately expanded with the idea that anything was possible. Every part of my being resonated with what I saw until eventually, it became a deep inner knowing within me. For me, an inner knowing bypasses all faith and belief; it just is.

Looking back, I've realized that what the bag represented to me was in fact the Universe itself, where we are able to create miracles out of the invisible and bring them to light in the visible realm. The objects inside the bag represent the infinite possibilities available to us at all times. Well, guess what? Now, you are about to receive your own bag of miracles!

So are you ready to take this journey towards recognizing and attracting more miracles? If so, then welcome to *Easy Breezy Miracle!*

*Have you noticed that
when you are feeling good,
everything seems to just fall into
place with ease and grace?*

What is a Miracle?

Before we become miracle magnets, it is important for us to have a deep understanding of what a miracle is, and how to expand our ability to recognize one while it's happening in our life, no matter how small or large it may seem.

In the dictionary, a "miracle" is defined as *an effect or extraordinary event in the physical world that surpasses all known human or natural powers and is ascribed to a supernatural cause.*[1]

Although this is a great definition, the words used to define "miracle" suggest it as being a bit out of reach and almost impossible.

Having witnessed countless miracles in my life and in the lives of thousands of my clients, I've come to add to the current definition of a miracle as being *an experience a person attracts into their life as a direct result of being in alignment with the natural flow of life.*

---

[1] "Miracle" *Dictionary.com Unabridged.* Random House, Inc. 20 Oct. 2011. <Dictionary.com http://dictionary.reference.com/browse/miracle>

What Does Being in Alignment Mean?

Have you noticed that when you are feeling good, everything seems to just fall into place with ease and grace? You may find yourself attracting amazing new opportunities, situations, and people into your life that support your greatest vision of your life. Your desires begin to manifest left and right, almost as if out of thin air, with little to no effort. This all happens when we are in alignment.

Being in alignment requires us to transcend patterns of worry, fear, doubt, and lack (just to name a few) that we may be holding on to. Being in alignment simply means we are in a pure state of joy; our purpose in life is to experience ultimate joy. Many people have shared with me that they've forgotten how to be happy. This usually happens due to beliefs we may have internalized through family, society, media, etc.–beliefs that tell us that we must search outside ourselves for happiness. The fact is that joy is our true nature, and all we need to do is reach deep within and reconnect with our true selves.

Simply put, when we make our joy the number one priority in our lives, we begin to realign ourselves with the flow of life, where we create fertile ground for miracles.

I always get asked the question: "How do I connect with joy?" There are many ways to reconnect with the energy of joy, and I'm excited to share them with you!

Alignment and Control

A lignment is not about control, nor is it about letting go. Alignment is letting be. Life is here for us, not against us, and it has always been this way. The Universe always presents us with the highest and most extraordinary opportunities to experience the most satisfying and extraordinary lives. It's only when we try to control (control usually comes from a place of fear) every aspect of our lives, other people's lives, specific outcomes, etc., that we move out of alignment and back into patterns of struggle, lack, and limitation. If you are experiencing some of these energies in your life, simply use them as feedback and as opportunities to grow and guide you back into alignment.

To be in alignment is not a matter of changing the Universe in order for it to align with you; rather, it is a matter of changing yourself and your perceptions to align yourself with the Universe. Alignment entails a lot of trust, as opposed to fear, and it requires you to develop and maintain a demeanor of positive energy. All your knowledge of miracle processes will be fruitless without this important and necessary condition. Just remember to be easy with yourself, and remember that like life itself, alignment is a process that takes some practice, especially if you've been living a certain way for so many years. It is for this reason that I attach the word "miracle" to the word "processes."

Alignment and Perception

The fact of the matter is that not one day passes us by where we don't experience hundreds of miracles. The word "miracle" is relative to everyone. Those who view miracles as having to be over-the-top, otherworldly experiences that defy all logic may tend to not notice all the miracles happening around them.

On the other hand, those who can easily recognize the blessings in their lives even in the most seeming simple of things, like each breath they take, a beautiful sunset over the ocean, watching a bee pollinate a flower, a random stranger displaying a simple act of kindness, and so forth, usually tend to notice the abundance of miracles in their lives. With their awareness alone of even the smallest blessings, they somehow attract more miracles in their lives, to the point where even the seeming "otherworldly" kind of miracles begin showing up in their lives. And you'll probably notice that these people are almost always in a space of joy.

Alignment is the underlying, overarching purpose of the concepts and activities I am sharing with you. The miracles you will be able to attract to your life after reading this book will be nothing more (and nothing less) than manifestations of your degree of alignment with the Universe.

How This Book Works

I think we are ready to explore the 5 core foundations to anchoring more miracles: Self Love & Acceptance, Releasing Attachments, Being Present, Circulation, and Imagination. Consider these "miracle foundations" as the conceptual framework that you should perpetually refer to during your personal transformation. They should serve as a focal point for everything you do in your life, no matter how great or how small. Think of the 5 miracle foundations as the basis for Mary Poppin's positive demeanor; allow the concepts to flow through your life rather than letting them form a rigid set of rules.

Each of these miracle foundations will be accompanied by what I call "miracle processes," which are easy, breezy, step-by-step, how-to instructions on transforming ideas into actions. Miracle processes have a basis in both spirituality and science: the use of prayer beads and repeated, meditative motions are related to psychological theories of conditioning and reinforcement. Think of miracle processes as your magical bag of tools that should be both helpful and fun to use.

...allow the concepts to flow through your life rather than letting them form a rigid set of rules.

Miracle Foundation #1

Self-love & Acceptance

...what love really is...

Self-love & Acceptance

The absolute most important foundation for anchoring more miracles is Self-love & Acceptance. My clients always ask me the question, "How do I love and accept myself more?" Before we answer that, it's important to understand what love really is.

From an expanded perspective, love is having a deep awareness of knowing who you really are and where you really come from. Love is having the understanding that you are in fact the Universe in physical form, actually experiencing more of Itself through you, as you. True love, which is indeed a miracle, is never conditional, nor is it ever supposed to be difficult or painful. Anything that may have convinced you otherwise usually comes from attachments we've projected on to what we think love should be. Love is the energy that flows through you, me, the trees, animals, planets, galaxies, the Universes, everything, and beyond.

There are many ways love can be expressed. Romantic love, platonic love, family love, love for animals, and love for our planet can be just a few examples of how we express love. Even though we may express love in different ways, ultimately they all lead to the same One Love.

But how do we align ourselves with this One Love? A great start is to simply be intentional in making ourselves our number one priority in our lives. We make ourselves a priority by choosing to nurture and care for ourselves physically, emotionally, mentally, and in all ways. For so long, many of us have been taught to put others first, otherwise we are selfish if we don't. Unfortunately, by doing this, many of us end up giving so much that we become depleted. We literally begin operating on empty.

In this case, what often happens is that by giving to others from a space of depletion, we begin to resent those that we are giving to. We begin to expect things from them and always find ourselves disappointed because these people are not meeting our expectations. So basically, we begin presenting ourselves to those around us from not as high a space as we could.

When we consciously make it our priority to nurture and care for ourselves, we begin to feel more satisfied and complete. We no longer look outside of ourselves to fill some kind of void. Then, as we begin living our lives from this space, we are able to give so much more to all those around us by just being ourselves. We'll no longer have to put on a show or overcompensate with our giving in order to be liked. Our giving then comes from a space of overflow, because we've given to ourselves first. What a magical concept, right?

Here are some specific miracle processes that will allow you to also cultivate your instinctive sense of self-love. Always remember that the bottom line to loving and accepting ourselves is making the time and effort to nurture and care for ourselves on a daily basis.

The Miracle Shower

One of the simplest yet most powerful ways to attract more miracles into your life is to take a daily miracle shower. Just like you spend time each day brushing your teeth, bathing, and eating, setting time aside to take a miracle shower will greatly attract more miracles in your life. I would encourage you to spend about one minute three times a day doing the miracle shower exercise, for optimal results. However, if you spend even 30 seconds a day taking a miracle shower, you will highly magnify your ability to attract more miracles into your life. The wonderful thing about this exercise is that you can be anywhere while you do it.

The Miracle Shower Miracle Process

1. Take three deep relaxing breathes.

2. Start noticing in your awareness a beautiful golden cloud take shape in the sky right above you. (If you need to close your eyes to visualize this, please go ahead and do so)

3. Make sure your arms are uncrossed, relaxed, and palms are facing up.

4. Start noticing golden white energy (the energy of miracles) drops pour out of the golden cloud over you. Notice every cell, fiber, and molecule of your being inside-out completely drenched in this beautiful golden white energy of miracles. See the golden white drops massage your mind and completely saturate it with the energy of miracles.

5. Notice that the golden white energy completely melts away any energy blocks within you (doubts, worries, stress, fears, etc) that might have prevented you from attracting miracles in your life.

6. When you feel like your shower is complete, open your eyes as you thank your beautiful golden cloud for blessing you with the energy of miracles.

The Smiling Heart

Smiling with our hearts is one of the most simple yet powerful miracle processes a person can do! When we smile with our hearts, an immediate energetic shift occurs within us that opens us up to the vast Divine Love flow of the Universe. Before entering a room or going out of the house, spend a few seconds focusing on your heart space, and try out the miracle process provided below. As you go out in the world, watch how quickly the energy changes in a room when you are in it, or how differently people respond to you.

You'll probably notice that the challenges or vibrations that come your way that once used to take a toll on you will no longer have the same affect they once had. You'll begin to attract the people and circumstances aligned with the new love vibrational energy you've created for yourself, which in turn leads to new opportunities, blessings, and miracles in your life.

The Smiling Heart Miracle Process

1. Spend a few seconds just focusing on your heart space.

2. For about 30 seconds, imagine what your heart would look like if it had a cute cartoon-like face smiling from ear to ear, showing as many teeth as possible.

You can even see some silly little faces that your heart makes to invoke the energy of joy.

3. Feel into the energy of gratitude for this moment of joy you created.

4. Ask your subconscious mind to remind you to smile with your heart periodically throughout the day. This will change the tone of your day.

Laughter

Have you ever heard the phrase 'Laughter is the best medicine?' Joyful laughter instantly raises the vibration of every cell and molecule of our being to soaring heights! Laughter aligns us with the flow of the Universe, and when we are in the flow, radiant beaming health and abundance in all areas of our lives become a daily occurrence.

Laughter connects us on a soul level to others, allowing for deeper connections to be made. It has even been scientifically documented that our cells begin to rejuvenate and operate at their optimum when we laugh. The more laughter we allow in our lives the more miraculous life becomes.

Laughter Miracle Process

1. Find a space where you feel comfortable making a bit of noise without feeling like you're disturbing anyone.

2. For at least 3-5 minutes each day, begin to laugh the way you might if you found something to be hysterically funny. At first it may feel a bit unnatural to you or maybe even a bit of a challenge, but just continue

with it. The more you practice the easier it will get. (If you are unable to self start your own laughter, find a funny video or think back to a time when you laughed really hard.)

Gratitude

Gratitude is one of the quickest and most powerful ways we can attract more miracles into our lives. Gratitude also has the ability to raise our emotional state which allows us to experience more joy, comfort, and love. A very important key to working with gratitude is being able to feel into the energy of gratitude. This is where a daily practice working with gratitude may be highly beneficial, because many of us might still need to develop our gratitude muscle. At first, it might feel like we are just going through the motions when we practice our gratitude, however over time gratitude will become second nature where we can easily connect with what it feels like to be grateful.

Gratitude Miracle Process

1. Every morning, after you've prepared yourself for the day and every night before you go to sleep, place your hands over your heart as you take 3 deep breaths.

2. Share at least 5 things you are grateful for out loud, and why you are grateful for them. I find that expressing a little passion behind my words really helps to connect me with the feeling of gratitude.

Examples:

I am deeply grateful for my 5 senses because I get to experience the many beautiful colors, textures, sounds, and fragrances around me.

I am grateful for my bed, because it provides me with an abundance of comfort.

I am grateful for the opportunity to share my gifts and talents with others, because it allows me to experience creative satisfaction.

I am grateful for my friends, because they see me for who I really am.

I am grateful for experiencing optimum health in every cell, fiber, and molecule of my being, because it allows me to focus on the things I love most in life.

Celebrate Often

Taking the time to celebrate often magnifies the blessings and miracles in our lives. When we celebrate, we are sending a message out to the Universe letting It know that we are taking notice and appreciating the blessings in our lives. The Universe then immediately responds by sending us more blessings to celebrate. We don't just have to wait for special occasions to celebrate; we can celebrate a good day at work, a great chat with a friend, an accomplishment, etc.

Miracle Process for Celebrating Often

Each day of the week, write out at least 5 successes you've had that day. Here is an example:

5 Successes of the Day

1. Got to work 5 minutes early
2. Received a compliment on my wardrobe
3. Received a great insight of how to expand my business
4. Had a great lunch with a friend
5. Experienced 1 good laugh today

At the end of the week, read back over all your successes and treat yourself in a special way with the intention of celebrating you and your successes. You can celebrate by going out to dinner, getting a massage, purchasing something nice for yourself, and the list goes on. The key is to celebrate at least once a week if not more.

Miracle Foundation #2

Releasing
Attachments

...meaningful connections flourish...

Releasing Attachments

The concept of detachment is not as difficult as it may sound. Many of us may confuse an attachment with a connection. The biggest difference between the two is that a connection comes from a space of love, whereas an attachment has an element of control or fear around it, no matter how minute it may seem. We may notice ourselves being attached when we have a fear of losing that thing we are attached to. When this happens, we usually start focusing heavily on details of how, why, where, when, and who; and that's when we find ourselves trying to control the situation or the people involved in it.

When we release the need to know all the specifics of every outcome or situation, we are able to move back into a state of ease and grace. This is the state where miracles begin to show up in our lives. It's also here where meaningful connections to people, places, and things can flourish without the distractions of the attachment to them we may have once developed.

The miracle processes I am about to share in this section of the book are specifically designed to help you focus on attracting miracles by being open to what the Universe has to offer you. You are open when you don't limit your expectations when it comes to the good things that can happen in your life; you are open when there is no negative energy taking up space in your heart and cluttering your vision. When you are open, you are in alignment.

Miraculous Mantras

Mantras work with the idea that every word carries a specific vibration, and when certain words are used together in a repetitive manner along with specific intention behind them, the vibrations created from these mantras begin to anchor in the desired intentions that go along with the mantras into physical form. Mantras have been used all over the world for thousands of years, and continue to serve as a powerful tool of transformation, healing, and miracles. I've worked with mantras for many years, and attribute many of the miracles in my life to them!

There are many powerful mantras that you can start working with. You can also formulate your own mantras if that feels more comfortable for you. The key with mantras is to be very disciplined and consistent in doing them everyday, at least until your desired intention from each mantra comes to fruition. Mantras also have a unique ability to relax the mind and bring a person back to the present moment, which is the most powerful space to be in when choosing to attract more miracles in one's life.

Prior to chanting a mantra, I like to take a moment to reflect on the fact that millions of people before me chanted the same or a similar mantra. Being mindful of this amplifies the power of the mantra for me, because through my reflecting I'm actually connecting to the energy of all the people who came before me.

The following formula is my personal miracle mantra formula. Remember, if you feel guided to create your own miracle mantra formula, please do so.

You will also notice that I repeat each mantra 108 times. The reason for this is because I use a malla mantra necklace which has 108 bead counts on it. You can repeat your mantras as many times as you feel guided, however make sure you are at least spending a good 30 seconds on each mantra to set in motion the desired energy wave behind the mantra. Mantras can be compared to building a physical structure or great work of art. Each day, we build from where we left off the day before, and before we know it we have created a beautiful masterpiece. When working with mantras, give yourself at least 60 days until the miracles start entering your life.

My miracle mantra formula

- *Om gum ganapataye namaha* – clears obstacles
- *Thiru neela kandum* – resolves karmic lessons with ease and grace
- *Aham Prema* – expands the Divine Love within us
- *Om shreem maha l'akshmye namaha* – attracts prosperity in all areas of life
- *Om breez namaha* – attracts good fortune and abundance

You can also create your own mantras. I like to use the following:

> **"I am open and receptive to knock-my-socks-off miracles in all areas of my life"**

Affirmative Prayer

When we hear the word prayer, many of us immediately associate it with something that has to do with religion, and usually only ever even think to pray when we are in need of something. This is more of the old paradigm form of prayer.

The new paradigm of prayer is all about having an affirmative conversation with the inner Divine spiritual aspect of ourselves. When we pray affirmatively, we come from a place of deep intentional knowing that whatever we are praying about, is already happening or is on it's way soon to showing up in our life experience. Praying basically means to make an intentional choice without being attached to a specific outcome. This process opens us up to miracles and blessings beyond what we might have come up for ourselves. Praying in this way is much more powerful than praying from a place of neediness or desperation. By going within, we immediately move out of victim consciousness and back into our power, where it's much easier to create the life we desire most for ourselves.

Affirmative Prayer Miracle Process

1. Recognizing that you are One with everything.

Example: How amazing it is to know that there is only one life operating right now, and that is the life of the Universe.

This life is also my life, it's the life of the trees, the stars, the planets, every person, everything. From this space of Oneness...

2. Affirm your desire.
(Feel free to use any of the following affirmative statements)
> I am...
> Right now, the truth is...
> I have...
> I choose...
> I easily attract...
> I experience...

Example: I have optimum health in every cell, fiber, and molecule of my being.

3. Gratitude
Example: I am so grateful for knowing that through this prayer, the process of me experiencing optimum health is now set in motion and will start to show up in my life with ease and grace.

4. Release all attachments to specific outcomes
Example: With an open heart, I lovingly release this prayer out to the Universe, knowing that this manifests in my life is in alignment with my highest and greatest good. And so it is.

5. Witness
For about 10-20 seconds, use your inner eye to visualize your prayer in action.
Example: If you asked to experience optimum health, see every cell of your body completely whole while you are smiling and living life to it's fullest.

The Piggy Bank of Miracles

I enjoy this miracle process because it reminds me to connect with my inner child, and always gives me a great excuse to put in a special miracle request to the Universe.

The Piggy Bank of Miracles Miracle Process

1. Get a piggy bank that makes you feel good. My piggy bank happens to be of the Disney character Dumbo.

2. Save any monetary coins you find in your couch or on the ground at home, the store, etc... These coins are always reminders from the Universe of the abundant miracles that surround us.

3. Place your piggy bank in front of you. Close your eyes and place the coin you found over your heart and affirm out loud a deep desire you'd like to experience in your life. At the end of your affirmative request, add the phrase 'I choose this or something greater.'

4. Place your coin in your piggy bank.

(Note: This is a fun and easy process. When you have 'placed your order' to the Universe, it's important to let go of all attachments to specific outcomes. This will open you up to being pleasantly surprised.)

Notes of Forgiveness

Forgiveness is one the most powerful ways to clear the blocks and obstacles preventing us from attracting the kind of miraculous life we've always envisioned for ourselves. To For-give literally means to give forth and release all energies that are not conducive to your expansion process. Some of these energies include resentments, grudges, and anger that we might still be holding on to. When we allow the Universe to unburden us of these energies that no longer serve our greatest good, we move into a state of complete freedom where the energy of love, joy, and miracles reside! The following miracle process may be a bit challenging for some people, so be gentle with yourself. I suggest sending these cards out at a pace that feels comfortable to you, and build from there. This process will lift most dense energy we carry with us, creating more room for miracles to enter our lives.

Notes of Forgiveness Miracle Process

1. Make a list of every person and situation in your life that you feel still needs forgiving. A great indicator to know if you still need to forgive is if you still feel an emotional

charge when you think of those people or situations. If you feel completely neutral and are in a place where you can easily send them love in person or from afar, then you have truly forgiveness.

2. Create or buy some nice cards that are blank inside. Thank you cards also work well.

3. For each person or situation you thought of that still need forgiving, write what you appreciate and love most about them. Don't mention anything about forgiveness in your words, just write a note that expresses the feeling of love and appreciation.

4. After you write your note of love and appreciation, place the card over your heart space and repeat the following phrase 33 times: 'I forgive you, and I love you.' If you find your mind is resisting, you can say: 'I'm willing to forgive you, and love you.'

5. If you have the address of the person you wrote this card to, go ahead and send it to them from the post office or the nearest mail drop box. If you don't have their address or if you are writing the card to a situation that happened instead of a person, go ahead and drop it off at the mail box anyway. The act of you going to the post office and 'releasing' these cards is a physical symbol of your act of forgiveness. At this point, you will probably feel a bit of weight lifted off your shoulders, knowing that you have truly forgiven.

Simplify to Magnify

One of the most effective ways to attract more miracles in our lives is to simplify our surrounding space. It's natural that over time many of us accumulate what seems to be extra baggage whether it's on the emotional or material levels. After carrying this baggage for a while, many of us begin to define ourselves by it which in turn blocks us from seeing and experience the miracles all around us.

Simplifying our physical surrounding space at least every 6 months will make room for more miracles to enter our lives. Any material items that we have not used in over a year - whether it's clothes, paperwork, or anything else collecting dust, it's time to donate, sell, or get rid of! If there are a few objects that hold a special meaning for us, then of course we can find a place for them, however the less we are attached to the more room we create for new miracles to enter our lives.

Miracle Process

Twice a year (maybe during the Spring/Autumn seasons) go through your home/work space to see if there are things you have not been using. For the most part, if it has been over 6 months since you have used an object, then it's time to donate, sell, or get rid of it.

When we are present,
we are at our most powerful
and able to manifest our desires
the most quickly.

Miracle Foundation #3

Being Present

...aware and connected...

Getting Present

There are many wonderful books that speak in-depth about the importance of being present, so I will keep it easy breezy in this book.

It may sound silly to us when someone says, "Live in the present moment" because we may think that if we are somewhere physically, how could we not be present? In reality, many of us are rarely fully in the present moment, because we are always either thinking about the past or constantly planning the future. When we continuously dwell on and live in the past, what happens is that we recreate it as part of our present experience. Even though the people, places, and things from our past experiences may have come and gone—in fact, even if they no longer exist—if we are perpetually reliving them in our present reality, they make up not just our past, but they become our present reality as well.

On the other hand, there are some people that always focus on the future by looking for the next thing to satisfy them. What I've noticed is that many of these people are rarely satisfied, because they aren't able to enjoy their present experience long enough due to the fact they are constantly looking towards the next thing to satisfy them.

When we are present, we are at our most powerful. It's in the present moment where we are able to manifest our desires the most quickly. Many of the miracle processes in this book also double as processes that teach us how to be in the present moment. Some of these processes include connecting with nature and being aware of our 5 senses.

A simple process I use to remind me to get present is setting my cell phone alarm clock to a different time each day. In my case, I enjoy fun numbers like 11:11am, 12:34pm, 3:33pm, etc. I usually set my alarm to a fun ring tone/song that makes me smile. After setting my alarm in the morning, I just continue on with the rest of my day. When the alarm goes off, I use it as a reminder to immediately get into my 5 senses for 1 minute or so. By making a conscious effort to be aware of what I see, hear, taste, smell, and touch, I'm not just physically being where I am, but I become physically, and consequently spiritually, present. This fun little process has taught me, over time, how to move out of the hustle and bustle that we tend to get caught up with each day, and how to take time out to get present. Ultimately, being present has allowed me to be more relaxed and open to the flow of life. Here are some specific miracle processes to aid you in getting present.

Breath Work

Taking the time to be intentional with our breathing has a tremendous effect on the body, mind, and spirit. Because many people have not properly been taught to breathe, they tend to have shallow breathing. Shallow breathing is usually found in someone who has a more anxious or stressed nature.

By simply re-teaching ourselves to take deeper and fuller breaths, we open ourselves up to miraculous transformation. First, by taking a few seconds a day to focus on our breath, we anchor ourselves in the present moment. It's in the present moment where we are able to connect with infinite possibilities anchoring them into our experience from the invisible to the visible realm. Second, taking deeper breaths relaxes us on every level which puts us back into alignment with the natural flow of life where miracles thrive.

Breath Work Miracle Process 1

1. Simply begin to observe your current breathing pattern.

2. Begin to shift your breathing pattern so that you breathe in for 3 counts, hold it for 1, and breathe out

for 3 counts. Begin with 1 minute a day, and add 1 minute each day until you've reached 11 minutes a day of this breathing pattern.

3. Maintain at 5 minutes per day once full 11 minutes has been achieved.

Breath Work Miracle Process 2 (advanced)

1. Simply begin to observe your current breathing pattern.

2. Begin to shift your breathing pattern so that you breathe in for 5 counts, hold it for 1, and breathe out for 5 counts. Begin with 1 minute a day, and add 1 minute each day until you've reached 11 minutes a day of this breathing pattern.

3. Maintain at 5 minutes per day once full 11 minutes has been achieved.

Observe how you begin to feel in the coming days and weeks ahead.

Changing Routine

Sometimes, a simple reason to why we are not experiencing the miracles we seek is simply due to a lack of variety in our daily routine. Sometimes, when we get comfortable in the same daily routine, stagnancy can manifest. It's always good to change up our routine, because it allows the Life Force energy to flow even more within us creating continual expansion. Changing our routine could be as simple as taking a different route to work, working out at different times of the day, waking up at different times in the morning, and having a cup of tea today instead of coffee. These are just examples.

Changing our routine can involve bigger things like trying something we've always wanted to but have hesitated on because of our fear around it. This could be something like public speaking, placing your art in a gallery, traveling the world, (well you get the picture.) Getting ourselves out of the routine and comfort zone, expands us into opportunities and experiences that we might not have experienced otherwise.

Miracle processes to changing up our routine

1. Travel
2. Taking a different way home from work

3. Trying new activities
4. Listening to different music
5. Thinking outside the box
6. Stepping into our power by overcoming our fear around something we've always wanted to try (public speaking, singing, flying a plane, etc)

Surrounding Yourself
with Bright Colors

Surrounding ourselves in bright radiant colors has an instant positive effect on our energy, mood, and overall wellbeing. Colors have been used in the healing arts for thousands of years. You may have noticed that most successful restaurants use the colors yellow, orange, or red in their logos, because they know that these colors stimulate the appetite. Each color holds a different vibration and plays in important part in how we are experiencing our life. Bright colors tend to raise our vibration and make us feel good. When we feel good, it means we are in the flow which opens us up to even more miracles.

Miracle process 1

Take a quick inventory of all the colors of the clothes in your closet. Are you wearing bright luminous colors or are they more mute and dull? Begin to add brighter colors to your wardrobe and over the next few weeks check out how you feel.

Miracle process 2

Adding vibrant colors to your living or work space also greatly shifts the vibration of your home. Be bold and try colors that make you feel good.

Examples:
- Painting 1 wall of a room a bright color
- Bright Furniture
- Colorful accessories (pillows, lamps, picture frames, vase)

Natural Fragrances/Essential Oils

Our sense of smell is a powerful gift that has the ability to alternate how we feel in an instant. Close your eyes right now and imagine yourself smelling a fully blossomed Gardenia flower. Different scents have the power to affect us in many different ways. Scents can relax us or they can excite us. Either way, fragrances that smell good to us have the gift of making us feel joyful instantly. Which again, when we are able to connect with pure joy, we are opening ourselves up to even more miracles life has in store for us.

Miracle Process

1. Find a natural fragrance or essential oil that smells amazing to you. If you can't find one, find a flower that smells great to you.

2. Place a tiny drop of the fragrance or oil at the tip of your nose so that scent stays with you for a while.

3. Enjoy the rest of your day.

Connect with Nature

Nature has the extraordinary ability of moving us back to our core center where we feel most grounded. If we find ourselves overwhelmed with what's going on in our lives, making some time to connect with nature is always nurturing for the soul. Nature has the gift of absorbing and unburdening us of the heavier vibrations we may be holding on to. Spending time out in nature lightens our loads which gives us the clarity to move forward in our lives with ease and grace.

Miracle Process

There are many ways we can connect with nature. Here are just a few suggestions:

1. Laying on the grass with shoes off

2. Camping with friends

3. Taking peaceful walks in a park

4. Hiking on a fun trail

5. Sitting under a tree while reading a book

6. Swimming at the beach

Flower Power!

D id you know that flowers hold some of the purest and most sacred energies on the planet? Flowers are revered by cultures all over the world for their miraculous healing and transformative properties. When flowers are placed in certain spaces, the vibration of the space immediately raises and shifts! Have you ever noticed how your mood instantly lightens up when you walk through a beautiful flower garden? If you are really intuitive, you will even feel the flowers connect with you and serve to assist you on an energetic level. If your home is feeling a bit dense or stagnant, place flowers all throughout the house and notice how fast the vibration shifts.

Flowers also surround us with the energy of fun and play, reminding us to let go of the worries and stresses we might be carrying as we relax into the present moment. I know since working with flowers, I have noticed that I am more balanced, energetic, and joyful, which of course have all set the perfect tone for even more miracles to enter my life.

Flower Power! Miracle Process

1. Choose flowers that make you feel good. If you can get potted flowers, that's even better as they will last a great deal longer.

2. Place the flower(s) over your heart space, and feel your love and gratitude for the flowers.

3. Thank the flowers for blessing your life and attracting more miracles into your life.

4. Place the flowers where you they can greet you every-day.

Friendship with the Sun

Since ancient times, the sun has been revered as one of the most potent sources of healing and transformation. The sun has the power to instantly raise our physical, emotional, and mental vibrations to their most optimum state. In many indigenous cultures, the Sun was prescribed as medication to heal many ailments, and is still used in many cultures today. The sun works on our deepest cellular level and returns us back to our most authentic and Divine Self. Of course, when we are operating from our most authentic self, it means we are in alignment with our purpose and the flow of the Universe creating the perfect environment for miracles to bless every area of our lives.

The following exercise can be done anytime the weather permits, and of course the more you work with it the more profound the shifts in your life will be. This exercise not only attracts more miracles into your life, it balances out your mood so that over time you are consistently operating from a space of joy.

Friendship with the Sun Miracle Process

1. Find a comfortable place outside where you can connect with the sun for about 5-10 minutes. It can be

your back yard, a park, a balcony, beach, or any other space where you will not be disturbed.

2. It's important to do this exercise either earlier in the morning or in the late afternoon to avoid the peek times of the Sun. The best times I've found are between 7-10am and after 4pm

3. Open your arms wide, and face up towards the sun with your eyes closed.

4. Take a moment to feel the warmth of the sun kiss your face.

5. Affirm three times "I am open and receptive to knock-my-socks off miracles in all areas of my life" and after the third time just add 'And so it is."

6. Place your right hand over your heart and left hand over it as you thank the sun for providing such healing, comfort, and rejuvenation in your life.

Miracle Foundation #4

Circulation

...as we give, we receive...

Circulation: Giving = Receiving

It's important to have a high sense of awareness and appreciation of the miracles that constantly enter our life no matter how small or large they may seem, so that the Universe can bless us with even more. But an even more powerful way to attract miracles into our lives is to create them for others.

Many of us think we have to wait for miracles to happen or that they happen outside of our power. This idea has been ingrained within us for centuries, completely moving us out of our true power and into victim consciousness. What we don't realize is that creating miracles in the lives of others puts us in a position of power. When we practice giving out of a space of joy, self-love, and freedom, we not only make others feel good but we feel good about ourselves too. We not only move back into our power by being the creator of our life, we also open the floodgates of miracles and prosperity to enter our lives because of something called the Principle of Circulation. Just like we have the Principle of Gravity which states what goes up must come down, the Principle of Circulation always creates a balance between giving and receiving. Eastern spirituality calls this Karma, while science might refer to this as Newton's 3rd Law, the Law of Action-Reaction. When we give, the Universe gives back.

Learning how to give is not necessarily a matter of improving your personality or reflecting upon your core values, it's simply about approaching your life with a scientific principle that says: as we give, so shall we receive.

The following miracle processes are simple, effective, and most of all, fun ways to tap into the flow of miracles that circulates the Universe. These miracle processes are not only some of the most interactive in this book, but they also bring about tangible and palpable results faster.

Miracle Love Drops

The Miracle Love Drops process is one example of using our imagination to attract more miracles.

Miracle Love Drops Miracle Process

1. Find a comfortable chair to sit on or bed to lie on.

2. Gently take 3 breaths and center.

3. Close your eyes and see yourself at one of your most favorite locations on the planet.

4. Notice that the sky is absolutely clear and blue.

5. Begin to notice beautiful heart-shaped objects start to fill the sky. As you take a closer look at the hearts, you begin to notice that they are filled with luminous liquid light energy.

6. Think of a situation, person, place, or thing that you'd like to bless with more miracles. That of course includes you.

7. Begin to see the hearts gently move closer to that which you are blessing with more miracles.

8. Now, see an abundance of these hearts drop over the situation, person, place, or thing that you'd like to

bless with more miracles. As the hearts move over what you're blessing, see them burst with liquid light (generally a bright golden white, pink, purple, or blue color) and saturate every part of that which you are sending this miracle to.

9. When you feel complete, please send the energy of gratitude to the Universe for this miraculous gift you have been able to give.

Miracle Cards

A fun and simple way to attract more miracles into our lives and in the lives of others is to create and share miracle cards. Most of us know about the power of intention, which basically states that what we focus on expands. This miracle process combines the power of intention and the power of circulation (giving and receiving) which I mentioned earlier in the book. I created this miracle process a few years ago, and the results have been jaw-dropping! By creating these miracle cards, we move ourselves out of the idea that we have to wait for miracles to happen and move into the idea that we indeed can create miracles. When we give and share with others freely without expecting anything in return, the Universe blesses more than we can comprehend.

Miracle Cards Miracle Process

You should be able to create at least 6-12 miracle cards out of 1 sheet of regular computer paper. Each card should be a little smaller than a business card. You can either type the wording on each card to make it look more professional, or you can write and draw it yourself.

1. On the front side of the card, using about an 18-24 font size, write the word 'Miracle Card.' You can make it as simple or as colorful as you like.

2. At the bottom of the front side of your card, using about an 8-10 font size, write the phrase 'Blessed with the energy of miracles.'

3. On the back of your card, using about an 8-10 font size, you can write something like 'Whoever receives this miracle, will begin to experience more miracles in their lives! And so it is...'

4. After you have finished writing all the wording, print out as many sheets, and find a local printer shop to laminate them for you. This is usually inexpensive and will add a very professional touch to your card.

5. Once your sheets are laminated, go ahead and cut them into small little pieces so that you now have little miracle cards.

6. So now, take your cards and place them over your heart space, and just affirm out loud 3 times 'Whoever receives these miracle cards will begin to experience more miracles in their lives, and so it is.'

7. There are to ways to give and share these miracles with others. You can either place them in different places where you know someone will see it (ie: supermarket, the mall, at work) or if you feel guided you can personally give the cards out as a random act of kindness.

The Phone Book of Miracles

One day, like most people I received yet another phone book at my front door. Since phone books are updated so often, many of us receive at least 2-3 new copies a year. As I was picking up the phone book, I immediately felt an overwhelming sensation of joy come all over me. In that moment I received an insight that in my hands was the opportunity to randomly help brighten the day of other people's lives, inspiring and showing them that there are people out there who care and genuinely want them to be happy.

How does this relate to miracles? Well, like many other processes I share in this book, this process deals with the concept that when we give from our hearts without expecting anything in return, the Universe immediately responds by blessing us in ways we would have never even been able to come up with ourselves. Anytime we feel stuck or in a mindset of lack, by giving we can quickly move out of these energies and open ourselves up to the vast miracles the Universe is constantly blessing us with.

Miracle Process

1. Find a phone book, and if you don't have one you can easily go online and find your local white pages.

with your eyes closed, open up the phone book to a random page.

3. Using your index finger and with your eyes still closed, move your finger around on the pages until you feel intuitively guided to stop.

4. Open your eyes and see the name your finger landed on. This will be the person you selected.

5. Create or purchase a beautiful card. It can be a thank you card, or it can just be blank on the inside.

6. Write the following inside the card:

7. "Please accept this random act of kindness from the heart, and always remember that you are absolutely extraordinary! May you continue to always be blessed with joy, love, and miracles in every area of your life! Thank you for being you. - The Universe."

8. If you feel guided to place a gift in the card, please do so. Some examples would be (gift certificates, small crystal stones, etc.).

9. When you send these acts of kindness in the mail, it is preferable that you don't put a return address as this shows that you are able to give freely from your heart.

Car Windshield Gifting

Another process similar to the Phone Book of Miracles process is the Car Windshield Gifting process. Again, this process works with the idea that when we give, the Universe gives right back to us.

Car Windshield Gifting Miracle Process

1. Find an empty parked car.

2. Create or purchase a beautiful card. It can be a thank you card, or it can just be blank on the inside.

3. Write the following inside the card:

   "Please accept this random act of kindness from the heart, and always remember that you are absolutely extraordinary! May you continue to always be blessed with joy, love, and miracles in every area of your life! Thank you for being you. - The Universe."

4. To take this process even further, and to attract even more miracles, place money in the card. I find that many people feel uncomfortable using this process and immediately go into a place of lack. However, the biggest breakthroughs I've had with clients is when

they used this process. This process is a great indicator of how much we trust the Universe. If you are having a hard time with this process, be gentle on yourself and ease into it.

Miracle Foundation #5

Imagination

Our ability to use our imagination is one of the greatest gifts we have been blessed with!

The Power of Imagination

Do you remember as a child when we were urged to use our full imagination and dream big? Many of us where told that the sky was the limit and we could do and be anything we wanted! Then, as we began to get a little older, many of us for some reason internalized beliefs that "using our full imagination is a waste of time" or "using our imagination is childish."

Well, one of the most important factors to creating and attracting desired miracles in our lives is to use our imagination. Our ability to use our imagination is one of the greatest gifts we have been blessed with! It's through our imagination that we manifest from the invisible into the visible. If we briefly think back on all the greatest inventors, artists, and visionaries, we will find that they didn't hesitate to use their imagination. I would say that each of us is our own inventor and artist, all we need is the attitude of not limiting ourselves to possibilities that the Universe might have in store for us. It's an attitude of believing that "just because something doesn't exist doesn't mean it can't."

Rediscovering your imaginative nature through these miracle processes will open you up to more miracles and more transformations than ever before!

...the realm of infinite possibility...

Creativity

Another important key to attracting more miracles in our lives is to get creative. Being creative activates the right side of the brain and the higher heart which are where our spirit communicates to us through the intuition. Being creative moves our mind out of the energy of limitation, and expands us into the realm of infinite possibility. It's in this realm of pure infinite possibility where Divine insights, revelations, ideas, and seeming miracles are birthed. By working with our gift of creativity, we open ourselves up to manifesting from the invisible to the visible.

Think about some of the great inventors of our time. By using their creative mind, they opened themselves up to receive ideas that would come to be known as some of the most transformational technologies and inventions of our times.

Some examples of getting creative:

Writing

Painting/Drawing

Inventing

Singing

Dancing

Playing an instrument

Thinking outside of the box

Designing

Creativity Miracle Process

For at least 30 minutes a day, set some time aside to focus on doing something creative. The mind might try to create distractions such as "I'm too busy" or "this is a waste of time" so know that this is normal and means that big breakthroughs will soon follow if you commit to being creative daily.

The Power of Music

Have you ever experienced that special moment when you hear a song and every hair on your body immediately stands up as chills consume every part of your being? Usually in those moments, we are in an expanded state where we feel connected to everything while our hearts are completely open.

When we are in this extraordinary space of bliss, we become magnets to miracles.

(Feel into the music.)

The Power of Music Miracle Process

1. Create a play list of songs that you know hold a special meaning to you, or songs that always make you 'feel like soaring' is how I like to describe it. The more songs the better, so that you won't get tired of listening to the same songs.

2. I find that using headphones magnifies this experience, so if you have them, I highly recommend them.

3. Find a comfortable and special place where you will not be disturbed.

4. If you have the ability to shuffle your song selection,

I highly recommend it, as the element of surprise will greatly assist this process.

5. Close your eyes, play the music, breathe into the energies the music provides for you.

6. To continue feeling into the music, combine this miracle process with gratitude.

The Miracle Dance!

One of my favorite miracle processes is dancing! Dancing works it's magic by literally moving stagnant energy in the body, mind, and energy field as it opens us up to the natural flow of Universal Life Force Energy.

Dancing also amplifies our energy field at least 1,000 fold, which easily attracts more miracles into our lives! As a bonus, Dancing builds up a person's confidence, and serves to assist in restoring optimum health.

The Miracle Dance! Miracle Process

Step 1: Spend 30 seconds - 1 minute stretching your legs and body.

Step 2: Set the intention to release all energies that are not serving your greatest good such as worry, stress, and any other cares held in your body and mind through your dancing.

Step 3: Dance like it's the best day of your life! The more carefree and fluid you are with your body, the more powerful of an experience this process will be,

and of course it's always nice to have some music playing!

The Energy of Play

For some reason, society has made us believe that as adults we can no longer play with toys we once used to as children. Many would be quick to tell you that it's a waste of time, irresponsible, and childish. However, this couldn't be farther from the truth.

Toys symbolize the energy of fun and play. When we are playing and having fun, usually we are moving ourselves into the vibration of joy. Joy is ultimately what everyone wants to experience, and why would we deprive ourselves of anything, especially a fun way that can move us into this space? It has been shown that when a person is happy, their body and mind relaxes which means they are in alignment and can flow with life, which of course is the very definition of what a miracle really is.

The Energy of Play Miracle Process

1. Think back to a toy that you used to play with as a child that evokes joyful memories for you. (It can be a doll, Lego building blocks, etc..) For me, it's a mini trampoline.

2. Purchase the same or similar toy, and place it somewhere in your home or work environment where you

can see and enjoy it everyday. The purpose of this is to evoke that feeling of joy from within you on a consistent basis.

3. A few times a week, play with the toy as you would have done as a child.

Cup of Faith & Miracles

This powerful miracle exercise builds a powerful inner-knowing on the deep subconscious level that miracles can and do exist. Many of us have heard over the past few years about the Law of Attraction and how what we intend and believe comes to fruition. Although this is true, many people still have a really hard time believing in this concept, because what they want and what is showing up in their life are completely two different things. The major point that the books and teachings about the Law of Attraction miss are the understanding that we have a conscious and subconscious mind. Quantum Science has discovered that 90% of our experience is a projection from our subconscious mind, while only around 10% from our conscious mind. So when a person thinks they want something and they are not seeing it manifest in their life, it's usually because there is a subconscious (unconscious) belief they might have internalized through television, ancestors, and society that is not aligning with their conscious desire or want.

What this simple exercise does, is it immediately triggers the subconscious mind with the idea that miracles can and will happen consistently, giving a person this knowing on a deep level which then allows for the miracles to manifest into their life experience.

Cup of faith & Miracles – Miracle Process

Step one: Find a colorful cup or mug that makes you feel good. The brighter the colors and more decorative, the quicker it will be for the subconscious mind to internalize what this cup symbolizes.

Step two: Write the words 'Faith & Miracles' on your cup with a permanent marker.

Step three: Every time you are at home, make sure to drink from your cup of faith & miracles.

Step four: For at least 30 days, before you take your first drink from your cup set the intention that with each sip/drink your take, your faith in attracting miracles is magnified 1,000 fold. The initial 30 days is just a loading period that allows the subconscious mind to automatically remember that when you drink from your special cup, miracles will surely follow.

Sweet Crystal Dreams

Another beautiful miracle process is something I like to call Sweet Crystal Dreams. It has been documented that crystals have been used in Energy Medicine as vibrational remedies for many centuries by many cultures. Crystals are not only stunning to look at, they each hold metaphysical properties that serve as change facilitators with the ability to restore physical, emotional, mental, and spiritual balance. There are many wonderful books that share the unique transformative properties of crystals, so I invite you to read up on the crystals that resonate with you most.

The following miracle process is a fun and simple way to attract more miracles in your life!

Sweet Crystal Dreams Miracle Process

1. Check in with yourself to see what you are looking to attract more of. It could attracting more financial abundance, romance, physical healing, joy, etc...

2. Find a crystal that matches the energy of the specific vibration you are looking to attract more of. For example: a Rose Quartz, Rhodochrosite, and Rhodonite all have to do with love. So if you are seeking to attract

more love in your life, then these crystals would be highly recommended.

3. Find a crystal that you resonate with. The best way to know if a crystal feels good to you, is to actually hold it with your left hand (the receiving hand) as your palm is closed. You will most likely know immediately if you resonate with a crystal, because you will either feel a pull towards it, feel some form of tingle sensation as you are holding it, and maybe even a subtle energy shift in your awareness.

4. Once you have decided on your crystal(s), hold it with your left hand palm closed, and set your intention of what miracle you would like this crystal to assist you in attracting.

5. Place the crystals inside and under your pillow case, and just leave it there until your miracle comes to fruition.

*Note, if you are highly sensitive, there are certain crystals that can be a bit too strong to place under your pillow right away, so gently work your way up to it. Pay attention to your dreams, because they will definitely be a great indicator of the shifts that are happening for you on an energetic level.

Connecting with the Healing Arts

The healing arts are all about connecting with modalities that enhance the well-being of our life. Whether we choose to receive a massage, Energy Healing, Nutrition Counseling, Acupuncture, or another type of holistic modality, the core intention of these therapies is to make us feel better. When we feel better, we are happier and more in alignment which opens us up to even more miracles.

Miracle Process

1. Affirm out loud to the Universe to attract into your life the holistic modality that would serve you for your greatest good at this time.

2. Just observe over the coming days and weeks what begins showing up for you. You may find that you come across different modalities that you resonate with.

3. Once you find something you resonate with, try it out and see how it feels to you. When you find a practitioner and modality that you enjoy, add it to your routine at least 1 a month as part of your self care practice.

...allow Easy Breezy Miracle *to help you get back to a state of pure joy; or let it help you simply maintain that state.*

Your Miracle Plan

...attracting more miracles...

Living Life the Easy, Breezy Way

The pages of this book have come to an end, yet that doesn't mean that the thoughts and processes contained herein have ended as well.

Don't leave this book on a shelf just because you have finished reading it. After all, it was meant to be your compact field guide towards living a more aligned and more miraculous life. Take it with you everywhere, and refer to it whenever you feel like it. Perhaps you're bored on the commute home, or need to take a break from a stressful day at the office—wherever you may be, or whatever emotional state you may be in, allow Easy Breezy Miracle to help you get back to a state of pure joy; or let it help you simply maintain that state.

Feel free to share this book with your friends and family, as I have shared it with you. As you know, circulation after all is a powerful principle that works in beautiful ways that we will never fully comprehend.

Also, feel free to make this book personal. Choose the miracle processes that you feel best keep you in alignment with the Universe. Feel free to write personal notes and thoughts on pages you have found particularly helpful, and feel free to think up your own creative miracle processes—I would love to hear from you!

To help you get started on attracting more miracles right this minute, I've created a 1 month sample miracle plan. I recommend switching up your miracle plan every two weeks to a month to keep it fun and fresh.

JANUARY	
SUNDAY 1	
MONDAY 2	Gratitude Upon Rising *Breath work during lunch break *Celebrate 5 successes of the day before bed
TUESDAY 3	*Gratitude Upon Rising *Miracle Dance for 15 minutes
WEDNESDAY 4	*Gratitude Upon Rising *Breath work during lunch break *Celebrate 5 successes of the day before bed
THURSDAY 5	*Gratitude Upon Rising *Share Miracle Cards throughout the day
FRIDAY 6	*Gratitude Upon Rising *Breath work during lunch break *Celebrate 5 successes of the day before bed
SATURDAY 7	*Celebrate successes of the week & do something special for self

Sample plan – Week 2

JANUARY	
SUNDAY 8	
MONDAY 9	Gratitude Upon Rising *Breath work during lunch break *Celebrate 5 successes of the day before bed
TUESDAY 10	*Gratitude Upon Rising *Miracle Dance for 15 minutes
WEDNESDAY 11	*Gratitude Upon Rising *Breath work during lunch break *Celebrate 5 successes of the day before bed
THURSDAY 12	*Gratitude Upon Rising *Share Miracle Cards throughout the day
FRIDAY 13	*Gratitude Upon Rising *Breath work during lunch break *Celebrate 5 successes of the day before bed
SATURDAY 14	*Celebrate successes of the week & do something special for self

Sample plan – Week 3

JANUARY	
SUNDAY **15**	
MONDAY **16**	*Miracle Shower in the morning *Smiling Heart exercise through the day
TUESDAY **17**	*Miracle Mantras for 5 minutes
WEDNESDAY **18**	*Miracle Shower in the morning *Smiling Heart exercise through the day
THURSDAY **19**	*Miracle Mantras for 5 minutes
FRIDAY **20**	*Miracle Shower in the morning *Smiling Heart exercise through the day
SATURDAY **21**	

Sample plan – Week 4

JANUARY	
SUNDAY **22**	
MONDAY **23**	*Miracle Shower in the morning *Smiling Heart exercise through the day
TUESDAY **24**	*Miracle Mantras for 5 minutes
WEDNESDAY **25**	*Miracle Shower in the morning *Smiling Heart exercise through the day
THURSDAY **26**	*Miracle Mantras for 5 minutes
FRIDAY **27**	*Miracle Shower in the morning *Smiling Heart exercise through the day
SATURDAY **28**	

To Help You Plan...

Please use the empty calendars in the next few pages for your own personal miracle plan. This allows you to create a simple guide that keeps you on track. I recommend using a pencil when writing your plan out, so that you can change it at anytime you feel like switching it up

SUNDAY	
MONDAY	
TUESDAY	
WEDNESDAY	
THURSDAY	
FRIDAY	
SATURDAY	

SUNDAY	
MONDAY	
TUESDAY	
WEDNESDAY	
THURSDAY	
FRIDAY	
SATURDAY	

SUNDAY	
MONDAY	
TUESDAY	
WEDNESDAY	
THURSDAY	
FRIDAY	
SATURDAY	

SUNDAY	
MONDAY	
TUESDAY	
WEDNESDAY	
THURSDAY	
FRIDAY	
SATURDAY	

SUNDAY	
MONDAY	
TUESDAY	
WEDNESDAY	
THURSDAY	
FRIDAY	
SATURDAY	

SUNDAY	
MONDAY	
TUESDAY	
WEDNESDAY	
THURSDAY	
FRIDAY	
SATURDAY	

SUNDAY	
MONDAY	
TUESDAY	
WEDNESDAY	
THURSDAY	
FRIDAY	
SATURDAY	

SUNDAY	
MONDAY	
TUESDAY	
WEDNESDAY	
THURSDAY	
FRIDAY	
SATURDAY	

SUNDAY	
MONDAY	
TUESDAY	
WEDNESDAY	
THURSDAY	
FRIDAY	
SATURDAY	

SUNDAY	
MONDAY	
TUESDAY	
WEDNESDAY	
THURSDAY	
FRIDAY	
SATURDAY	

SUNDAY	
MONDAY	
TUESDAY	
WEDNESDAY	
THURSDAY	
FRIDAY	
SATURDAY	

SUNDAY	
MONDAY	
TUESDAY	
WEDNESDAY	
THURSDAY	
FRIDAY	
SATURDAY	

*Thank you for allowing me to
connect with you through the
words and energy of this book.
Here is to the abundance of
easy, breezy, miracles
about to enter your life!*

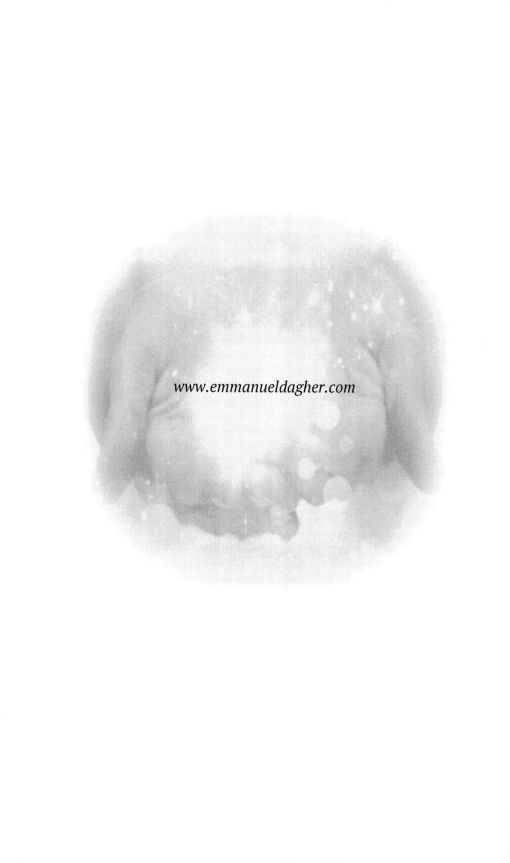
www.emmanueldagher.com

Continue the journey...

It has been such an honor to connect with you through *Easy Breezy Miracle!*

Let's continue on with our journey together and keep in touch. I would love to hear about your personal experiences using the processes from *Easy Breezy Miracle*, and all the positive shifts you manifest in your life as a result To share your feedback or to learn more about how you can create even more miracles in your life, please visit:

www.emmanueldagher.com

With love,
Emmanuel

*...blessed with
the energy of miracles...*

Made in the USA
San Bernardino, CA
14 February 2014